BREATHING ROOM

Pursuing a Pace That Will Finally Give You Peace

SANDRA STANLEY

Contents

To Andrew, Garrett, and Allie—

My greatest joys and the "great work"
for which I'm so grateful I did not come down.

{Nehemiah 6:3}

How to Use

BREATHING ROOM IN A GROUP

1 | **WATCH.**

As a group, watch the session video (15 minutes), viewable from the *Breathing Room* app or DVD.

2 | **DISCUSS.**

As a group, talk through the corresponding Discussion Questions found at the beginning of each chapter.

3 | **JOURNAL & DRAW.**

On your own time, journal your way through the week's devotions and challenges.

—————————◇◇—————————

Are you the Leader or Facilitator?

If you find yourself leading a group of friends or your Bible study group through the Breathing Room study, check out groupleaders.org/breathingroom for tips on how to lead the discussion for each session.

This book was supposed to be on shelves 12 months ago. To explain why it wasn't, I have to back up a decade.

When my oldest son, Andrew, entered high school, it dawned on me that I was in the latter part of my full-time, hands-on mom season. My three kids, who are close in age, would all be out of the house before I knew it. As the reality of that started sinking in, I began asking God to give me some vision for what was next. What would I devote my time and energy to once I'd washed the last baseball uniform and bought the last prom dress?

What God revealed was not at all what I expected. I wasn't the sort of mom who wanted to perpetually parent. *(This was about what I would do after my children moved out!)* And yet, God began to move my heart toward kids from difficult circumstances. I began researching and educating myself on all things foster care. Slowly, I gained clarity that this was the direction God was leading. So just a few months after Andy and I moved our youngest child into her dorm room, we moved our foster daughter into our home.

Around this same time, I was talking with the team that published my first women's study, *Comparison Trap,* about what would come next. I'd enjoyed the process of writing and filming that study and was excited about creating a second one. We were hearing amazing stories from women who'd been impacted by it. I was sure God would celebrate that success and give us wisdom for the next project. But every time I was on my knees, I would get a no from the Lord. I would feel a check in my spirit that maybe the timing wasn't right.

The team and I talked through some ways to lighten the workload, but still, God was giving me a no. I was back in the parenting trenches of helping with homework and driving our foster daughter all over town and was beginning the process of going back to school for my Master's Degree in Christian Studies. ***As it turns out, I just didn't have any breathing room to write a study about breathing room!***

It was a chance to practice one of the lessons we'll cover together in this book: I had to say *no for now, not for always.* Pausing the project wasn't what I expected to be doing, but God's *no* had become so clear that it was really an obedience issue. I needed to choose peace over progress.

Maybe you grabbed this book because you're facing a similar dilemma. Maybe you've already overwhelmed your calendar or drained your bank account in the pursuit of *more.* If so, you're not alone. The current of culture swallows up every spare minute and dollar it can.

Breathing room doesn't occur naturally. It will require practical changes in how you handle your time and money—which is why I hope you'll take advantage of the exercises that follow each daily devotion in this book. As we practice together over the next 28 days, I hope you'll discover the amazing benefits of living with margin. God didn't design us to go hard all day, every day. Instead, as we'll see in Scripture, he offers us not just breathing room, but a richer relationship with himself as well.

Thanks for coming along with me for the next few weeks as we opt out of the overwhelming pace and bring back our *breathing room.*

Sandra

1

FEARS

Bottom Line:

Don't trade your peace for progress.

DON'T TRADE YOUR

peace for progress.

VIDEO REFLECTIONS

....

....

....

....

....

....

....

....

....

....

....

....

....

....

1 | Which of the women in the opening video did you most relate to? Why?

2 | There are four fears that drive us to live without breathing room. Which do you struggle with most?

☐ Fear of Missing Out
☐ Fear of Not Mattering
☐ Fear of Falling Behind
☐ Fear of Disappointing Others

3 | Where are you currently sacrificing your peace (or your family's peace) for progress? Here are a few hints:

I _____ to try to keep up with _____ .

I _____ so he/she would think I was _____ .

4 | The Israelites were afraid they'd go hungry if they followed God's command to stop working for one day each week. Talk about a time when you were afraid to follow God. How did you respond?

5 | Creating breathing room begins by wrestling with the question, "Do I trust God?" In what area of life is it hardest for you to trust God? Do you currently have breathing room in that area?

THE LORD IS MY SHEPHERD, I LACK NOTHING. HE
MAKES ME LIE DOWN IN GREEN PASTURES, HE LEADS
ME BESIDE QUIET WATERS, HE REFRESHES MY SOUL. HE
GUIDES ME ALONG THE RIGHT PATHS FOR HIS NAME'S
SAKE. EVEN THOUGH I WALK THROUGH THE DARKEST
VALLEY, I WILL FEAR NO EVIL, FOR YOU ARE WITH ME;
YOUR ROD AND YOUR STAFF, THEY COMFORT ME.

Psalm 23:1–4

In the chaotic everyday pace of meetings, events, obligations, carpooling kids, caring for parents, serving others, finding "me time," running errands, running across town, running myself ragged, and running out of energy… I sometimes want to literally "lie down in green pastures" or sit "beside quiet waters." Though I'd settle for just a cup of coffee on the back porch.

We need breathing room.

David's words today remind us that's exactly what we'll find when we lean in and trust God. Just as a shepherd does for his sheep, God provides, guides, refreshes, and protects us. We can slow down and stop striving. We can lay aside our fears of missing out, falling behind, and disappointing others. We can trade our chaotic pace for the peace of living in line with God.

That probably sounds appealing. None of us enjoy living without any margin. But I know the pushback—maybe it's what you're thinking right now. *If I slow down, how will I get everything done?*

Look back at David's declaration, "The Lord is my shepherd, I lack nothing." Let this beautiful truth from David's song of trust reassure you. When the Lord is your shepherd, you will not lack. You can exchange your crazy pace for the deep breath that comes from trusting God with your calendar and your "to-do" list. It's a very good trade.

JOURNAL YOUR THOUGHTS

....

....

....

....

....

....

....

....

We can slow down and stop striving.

WHAT ARE YOU AFRAID OF?

In this week's video, we talked about a few common—but often undetectable—fears that can deplete us of our breathing room. How, specifically, have you seen these fears play out in your decision-making?

It may take some reflection, but try to write down examples for as many of the fears as you can. Uncovering these could be a game-changer.

☐ Fear of Missing Out
  Example: The concert tickets were really expensive, but I didn't want to miss a night out with the girls.

....

....

....

☐ Fear of Falling Behind
  Example: I've worked late every day this week to win favor with my boss.

....

....

....

☐ Fear of Not Mattering
Example: I felt like I wasn't contributing to our family financially, so I took on an extra job that consumes too much of my time.

....

....

....

....

....

☐ Fear of Disappointing Others
Example: I agreed to join the book club because I didn't want to say no to my friends.

....

....

....

....

....

For the rest of the day, before you commit to a new obligation or expense, ask yourself if any of these fears are driving your decision. Warning: brutal honesty may be required.

> REMEMBER THE SABBATH DAY BY KEEPING IT HOLY. SIX DAYS YOU SHALL LABOR AND DO ALL YOUR WORK, BUT THE SEVENTH DAY IS A SABBATH TO THE LORD YOUR GOD. ON IT YOU SHALL NOT DO ANY WORK, NEITHER YOU, NOR YOUR SON OR DAUGHTER, NOR YOUR MALE OR FEMALE SERVANT, NOR YOUR ANIMALS, NOR ANY FOREIGNER RESIDING IN YOUR TOWNS. FOR IN SIX DAYS THE LORD MADE THE HEAVENS AND THE EARTH, THE SEA, AND ALL THAT IS IN THEM, BUT HE RESTED ON THE SEVENTH DAY. THEREFORE THE LORD BLESSED THE SABBATH DAY AND MADE IT HOLY.
>
> *Exodus 20:8–11*

Do you remember curfew or some of the other rules your parents had for you as a teenager? If you were a typical teen, those restrictions probably felt arbitrary—like your parents were just trying to control you or catch you misbehaving. Your early impression of religion may have been (or perhaps still is) that God's rules are similar—randomly in place so he can catch you falling short of perfection.

I bet you can now appreciate the *reasons* for each of the rules your parents set. God's rules are the same way. When he commanded the Israelites to take a Sabbath, he had a good reason. He knew they would *need* rest. He created their bodies and their minds. He created our bodies and our minds. The Creator knows his creation. He knows we cannot go hard all day, every day, without hitting a wall. He knows we cannot possibly sustain a nonstop pace without breaks, without rest.

God designed us to need breathing room in our regular rhythm. And in this need for rest, we find a regular reminder that we need *him*. We need him to provide for us, without us working exhausting overtime hours. We need *him* to maintain our friendships through seasons when we must prioritize family. We need *him* to validate our worth apart from how our lives compare to our friends' lives.

Living at our limits leaves us needing God in a frantic, frenzied, desperate way. *God, rescue me. I'm exhausted!* How about we try the alternative of following God's Sabbath rule and letting him meet our needs while we experience the peace of a pace with breathing room.

JOURNAL YOUR THOUGHTS

LIVING AT YOUR LIMITS

Can you relate to feeling exhausted? Needing rest—physically or emotionally—is a reminder that we need God. Where are you living at your limits, in need of a break?

Write down a circumstance or situation that's exhausting you right now.

....

....

....

....

....

How does this circumstance remind you that you need God?

I need God to...

....

....

....

Complete this prayer with your own words.

God, this situation is exhausting me. I've been living at my limits for too long and I need a break. I'm ready for breathing room. I'm ready for peace.

....

....

....

....

....

....

....

....

....

....

....

....

....

....

DAY 3 DEVOTION

DO NOT WORRY THEN, SAYING, "WHAT WILL WE EAT?" OR "WHAT WILL WE DRINK?" OR "WHAT WILL WE WEAR FOR CLOTHING?" FOR THE GENTILES EAGERLY SEEK ALL THESE THINGS; FOR YOUR HEAVENLY FATHER KNOWS THAT YOU NEED ALL THESE THINGS. BUT SEEK FIRST HIS KINGDOM AND HIS RIGHTEOUSNESS, AND ALL THESE THINGS WILL BE ADDED TO YOU. SO DO NOT WORRY ABOUT TOMORROW; FOR TOMORROW WILL CARE FOR ITSELF. EACH DAY HAS ENOUGH TROUBLE OF ITS OWN.

Matthew 6:31–34 (NASB)

One thing I've learned about studying the Bible is to always look for repetition. The phrase *all these things* is mentioned three times in the second half of today's verses. That means it's significant! When Jesus was delivering the Sermon on the Mount, he knew his audience struggled with worry over what they would eat, what they would drink, and how they would clothe themselves. That's what *all these things* meant for them. Jesus let them know that although they worried over *all these things,* God was keenly aware of their needs. Jesus gently reminded them that if they would obey him wholeheartedly and remain focused on what really matters, their physical needs would also be met.

While we live in a completely different day and age, and we don't typically have to worry about what we're going to eat or what we're going to drink or even what we're going to wear, we have our own *all these things,* don't we? We have our own worries that distract and preoccupy us. Yet Jesus's principle still applies.

So, what are *all these things* for you? What are you worried about? What are you distracted by? What are the things you're striving for, seeking, spending tons of time on? Let's pause and reflect and return our attention to the place it belongs. If we seek first his kingdom and his righteousness—obey him and focus on what's truly important—*all these things* will be taken care of as well.

JOURNAL YOUR THOUGHTS

....

....

....

....

Jesus gently reminded them that if they would obey him wholeheartedly and remain focused on what really matters, their physical needs would also be met.

ALL THESE THINGS

The Israelites worried most about food, drink, and clothing. That might not translate to your situation. So let's figure out what worries may be stealing your breathing room.

What keeps you up at night?

....

....

....

Which worries are you trying to control with your time or money?

....

....

....

Which worries are leaking into your relationships?

....

....

....

Use some of the worries you've just identified to personalize what Jesus says in today's verse.

DO NOT WORRY THEN, SAYING,

"WHAT WILL _____?"

or

"WHAT WILL _____?"

or

"WHAT WILL _____?"

...FOR YOUR HEAVENLY FATHER KNOWS

THAT YOU NEED ALL THESE THINGS.

> BUT BLESSED IS THE ONE WHO TRUSTS IN THE LORD,
> WHOSE CONFIDENCE IS IN HIM. THEY WILL BE LIKE A
> TREE PLANTED BY THE WATER THAT SENDS OUT ITS ROOTS
> BY THE STREAM. IT DOES NOT FEAR WHEN HEAT COMES;
> ITS LEAVES ARE ALWAYS GREEN. IT HAS NO WORRIES IN
> A YEAR OF DROUGHT AND NEVER FAILS TO BEAR FRUIT.
>
> *Jeremiah 17:7–8*

When our kids were young and we wanted to help them overcome a fear, we practiced. A LOT. Diving into the deep end of the pool, confidently shaking an adult's hand, fessing up and asking forgiveness. My husband, Andy, even helped our daughter practice breaking up with her middle school boyfriend! As parents, we knew that the only way to help our kids overcome fear and become more confident was by practicing.

This formula applies to other fears too. The only way to overcome them is with practice. What does this mean for the fears that steal our breathing room? It means they are each a chance to practice trusting God. As we see God meet our needs despite our fears of missing out or falling behind, we grow more confident that he can be trusted. This is why—in the face of their very real fear of finding enough food—God established the routine of a Sabbath for the Israelites. Week after week, fear after fear, God was proving that he could be trusted.

In today's passage, Jeremiah describes what it's like to have earned such a confidence in God. He says that the person who trusts in the Lord doesn't have to fear hard times. She doesn't have to worry about the future. Those are two really good reasons to welcome the fears that try to steal our breathing room. Obviously, welcoming fears isn't easy—we're afraid, after all. But remember, our fears give us a chance to practice trusting God. And, eventually, our practice will make perfect.

JOURNAL YOUR THOUGHTS

....

....

....

....

....

As we see God meet our needs despite
our fears of missing out or falling behind,
we grow more confident that he can be trusted.

START WITH SCRIPTURE

Write, illustrate, or journal your thoughts about the following passage. Try today to memorize at least the first part, *"When I am afraid, I will put my trust in you."*

WHEN I AM AFRAID,

I WILL PUT MY TRUST IN YOU.

IN GOD, WHOSE WORD I PRAISE,

IN GOD I HAVE PUT MY TRUST;

I SHALL NOT BE AFRAID.

WHAT CAN MERE MAN DO TO ME?

Psalm 56:3-4

> BUT GOD DEMONSTRATES HIS OWN LOVE FOR US IN THIS: WHILE WE WERE STILL SINNERS, CHRIST DIED FOR US.
>
> *Romans 5:8*
>
> FOR GOD SO LOVED THE WORLD THAT HE GAVE HIS ONE AND ONLY SON, THAT WHOEVER BELIEVES IN HIM SHALL NOT PERISH BUT HAVE ETERNAL LIFE.
>
> *John 3:16*

So much of the fear we face is rooted in the age-old insecurity of not being enough. I don't matter enough. I'm not doing enough. I'm not good enough. I'm not smart enough. I'm not lovable enough. And it's true. We are not enough.

But God…

God, who knows every single thing about us—even the stuff we work so hard to hide—offers a way to be enough. He proves our worth by making an enormous sacrifice on our behalf. And because he wants to make sure we don't miss it, he keeps the message very simple.

For God so loved the world that he gave his one and only Son, that whoever believes in him shall not perish but have eternal life.

God is well aware of our inability to pay the debt for our sins. Because of his great love for us, he gave his Son to pay that debt. Again, he made our part so simple. Simply believe that Jesus' death erases our debt and receive a restored relationship with God.

God loved. God gave.
We believe. We receive.

Ladies, God believes that even the self-centered, sinful version of you is worth the unimaginable price of his Son's life. Stop your striving and rest. He has proven your worth once and for all.

JOURNAL YOUR THOUGHTS

....

....

....

....

....

....

....

YOU ARE ENOUGH

Where is the insecurity of not being enough leaving you without breathing room? What are you compensating for by trying harder or spending more? Fill in a few of the blanks below.

- I am not .... enough.

- I am not .... enough.

- I am not .... enough.

What would it look like to stop your *striving and rest* as it relates to each of these insecurities?

- ....

- ....

- ....

I PRAISE YOU BECAUSE I AM FEARFULLY
AND WONDERFULLY MADE; YOUR WORKS
ARE WONDERFUL, I KNOW THAT FULL WELL.

Psalm 139:14

DAY 6 DEVOTION

> DO NOT BE ANXIOUS ABOUT ANYTHING, BUT IN
> EVERY SITUATION, BY PRAYER AND PETITION, WITH
> THANKSGIVING, PRESENT YOUR REQUESTS TO GOD.
> AND THE PEACE OF GOD, WHICH TRANSCENDS
> ALL UNDERSTANDING, WILL GUARD YOUR HEARTS
> AND YOUR MINDS IN CHRIST JESUS.
>
> *Philippians 4:6–7*

Imagine a closet in complete disarray—dresses, jackets, jeans, shirts, and workout clothes all crammed in. There's a jumble of shoes, boots, and flip-flops on the floor. Purses are flung here and there. The suitcase contents from the last trip you took are spilling out of a bag in the back. Maybe you don't have to imagine. Maybe you can simply walk across the room and open a door—except you're a little bit scared you'll be sucked in and never heard from again!

While it's okay for your closet to be this way, it's not okay for your life to be this way.

You may be able to cram *just one more* hanger onto the rod. But cramming *just one more* commitment, or *just one more* purchase, or *just one more* project into an already bulging-at-the-seams schedule could be the *just one more* that takes you out. *Just one more* could steal the peace you long for or the patience you need for the people you love.

So can I make a suggestion? What if, when the next opportunity presents itself, you present it directly to your heavenly Father? You find a quiet place to steal away. You spend a few minutes thanking him for the amazing opportunities that come your way. And you let him tell you if your life has room for just one more. This pause will give you such clarity and peace, I promise. The beginning glimmers of breathing room are waiting on the other side of creating this habit.

JOURNAL YOUR THOUGHTS

....

....

....

....

....

....

....

....

....

....

....

....

JUST ONE MORE

Do you have any past examples of trying to add just one more and ending up in a mess because of it? *Just one more commitment… just one more purchase… just one more project.*

....

....

....

....

....

....

Are there any areas of life where you're currently maxed out, without any margin for *just one more?*

- ....

- ....

- ....

In the next few weeks, we'll be working through ways you can create and protect breathing room in those areas. Until then, try "closing the closet door" and resisting the temptation of *just one more.*

———◇◇———

Heavenly Father,

I'm so grateful for the time, money, and energy you've given me. Though I'm afraid I haven't used those gifts the way you want me to. I've stretched myself too thin and I see now that I'm on the brink of a mess. Please give me clarity to judge future opportunities and courage to obey when you show me that I don't have room for just one more.

....

....

....

....

....

....

....

....

> FOR THE WORD OF GOD IS ALIVE AND ACTIVE. SHARPER THAN ANY DOUBLE-EDGED SWORD, IT PENETRATES EVEN TO DIVIDING SOUL AND SPIRIT, JOINTS AND MARROW; IT JUDGES THE THOUGHTS AND ATTITUDES OF THE HEART. NOTHING IN ALL CREATION IS HIDDEN FROM GOD'S SIGHT. EVERYTHING IS UNCOVERED AND LAID BARE BEFORE THE EYES OF HIM TO WHOM WE MUST GIVE ACCOUNT.
>
> *Hebrews 4:12–13*

don't know about yours, but my lack of breathing room can come wrapped up in some pretty nice-looking packaging. I can convince myself that saying yes to something is really the prudent thing to do, what with how helpful I am to God and all. I can even deliver a great explanation to those around me who are giving me the side-eye. *This isn't a long-term commitment; I'm just helping her out in a pinch. It would be rude not to go. It's not really that expensive if you think about how often I'll use it.*

Truthfully, I know and God knows—and my side-eyed loved ones probably know too. By asking us to live with breathing room, God is offering us something better. He doesn't give rules because he wants something *from us.* He gives them because he wants something *for us.*

Are you trying to justify something that you know you should say no to in this particular season? Does wisdom whisper, "Not right now," but everything in you wants to pretend you don't hear? Trust me. Saying *no for now, but not for always* is a great place to land. It preserves your breathing room and your integrity.

We can trick ourselves. We can sometimes trick our people. But nothing in all creation is hidden from God's sight. He knows our thoughts and even sees the attitudes of our hearts. We might as well drop the charade, right? Let's pay close attention to God's loving instruction and watch him lead us to a place of peace, with space to breathe.

JOURNAL YOUR THOUGHTS

....

....

....

....

....

....

He doesn't give rules because he wants something from us. He gives them because he wants something for us.

IDENTIFYING OUR JUSTIFICATIONS

In which area of life are you most likely to justify living without breathing room?

☐ Time   ☐ Relationships

☐ Money   ☐ ....

How have you justified something in the past that you knew you should have said no to?

• *It's a special occasion. I can splurge just this once!*

• ....

• ....

• ....

• ....

Who is most often on the receiving end of your excuses?

☐ You

☐ Your family

☐ Your friends

☐ Your colleagues

☐ Your acquaintances

☐ ....

No for now, not for always

Rather than justifying a decision that's going to leave you in a mess, try reminding yourself that saying no for now is not saying no forever. You may have the margin to say yes to the same opportunity in the future or maybe to an even better one.

....

....

....

....

TIME

2

Bottom Line:

My time is limited, so I must limit what I do with my time.

MY
TIME IS
LIMITED, SO
I must limit
WHAT I DO
WITH MY
TIME.

....

....

....

....

....

....

....

....

....

....

....

....

....

....

....

1 | In the video, Sandra said, "The days might seem long, but the years truly are short." In your current season of life, how does this statement resonate with you?

2 | Below is a list of emotions you may experience when your calendar is short on breathing room. Which of these best describe how you feel when your schedule is maxed out?

Anxious	Sarcastic	Unfocused	Guilty
Tired	Stressed	Overwhelmed	Jealous
Frustrated	Bitter	Useful	Disappointed
Important	Energized	Helpless	

3 | Think about a recent busy day. Did any of these fears contribute to your overwhelming schedule? If yes, how?

☐ Fear of Missing Out
☐ Fear of Not Mattering
☐ Fear of Falling Behind
☐ Fear of Disappointing Others

4 | If someone looked at your weekly calendar—every hour—what would they say about how you're spending your time? Who or what is getting the most? Is that how you want this season of your life to be defined?

5 | What is one thing you can remove from your calendar this week to start practicing the truth that *my time is limited, so I must limit what I do with my time*?

> TEACH US TO NUMBER OUR DAYS,
> THAT WE MAY GAIN A HEART OF WISDOM.
>
> *Psalm 90:12*

The last roller coaster I rode was like most—a super slow start creeping up the incline and then, all of a sudden, the speed picks up and the remainder of the ride is crazy fast with all kinds of twists and turns.

Now let me just say that the wooden roller coaster experience for a limber, young 15-year-old is completely different than that of a 40-something-year-old who forgot she wasn't 15 and had to go directly to a chiropractor after the whole jerky experience... but anyway, I digress.

Time is so much like that roller coaster, isn't it?

Our early years seem to creep along at a snail's pace. We think we'll never be a teenager. Then we think we'll never be 16 and get a driver's license. Then we think we'll never be 18 and out the door to college. But alas, we get that far and things start to speed up. Pretty quickly, time flies by at an astounding clip.

When we wrap our minds around the reality that life is fast and we have a finite number of days, we see the need to use our time wisely. But not to *accomplish* more. Today's verse is not, "Teach us to number our days, that we may squeeze in every last thing on our 'to-do' list."

No, when we think about how to spend the time that's flying by so fast, it should be a call to get our priorities straight. We should start by asking: *Are the people and things that are most important to me getting first dibs on my time or are they getting the leftovers?*

Numbering our days means prioritizing who and what receives our time. We can only create breathing room once we've acknowledged that our time is limited, so we must limit what we do with our time.

JOURNAL YOUR THOUGHTS

....

....

....

....

....

....

....

Our time is limited, so we must limit what we do with our time.

MOST IMPORTANT

Let's answer the question, *Are the people and things that are most important to me getting first dibs on my time or are they getting the leftovers?*

Write down the names of the three people who currently claim most of your time.

1 | ....

2 | ....

3 | ....

If you want to give our time to the people who are *most important* to you, is there anyone on this list who doesn't belong? Is there anyone missing?

....

....

....

....

Write down the three activities or organizations that currently claim most of your time.

1 | ....

2 | ....

3 | ....

If you want to give our time to the causes that are *most important* to you, is there anything on this list you don't have a particular passion for? Is there anything missing?

....

....

....

....

....

....

THEREFORE, SINCE WE ARE SURROUNDED BY SUCH A GREAT CLOUD OF WITNESSES, LET US THROW OFF EVERYTHING THAT HINDERS AND THE SIN THAT SO EASILY ENTANGLES. AND LET US RUN WITH PERSEVERANCE THE RACE MARKED OUT FOR US, FIXING OUR EYES ON JESUS, THE AUTHOR AND PERFECTER OF OUR FAITH, WHO FOR THE JOY SET BEFORE HIM ENDURED THE CROSS, SCORNING ITS SHAME, AND SAT DOWN AT THE RIGHT HAND OF THE THRONE OF GOD. CONSIDER HIM WHO ENDURED SUCH OPPOSITION FROM SINFUL MEN, SO THAT YOU WILL NOT GROW WEARY AND LOSE HEART.

Hebrews 12:1–3

My grandmother lived to be 100 years old. She was born in 1911 and died in 2011. Think for a moment about the changes she witnessed: the Great Depression, numerous wars, indoor plumbing, television, paved roads, fast cars, airline travel, microwave ovens, computers, mobile phones, the Internet, and, get this, eighteen presidents—Taft through Obama. That's amazing to me!

In 1911, unlike today, there were limited options for how people spent their time. Most days, they stayed within a one-mile radius of home. When it got dark, everyone went to bed.

Instead of struggling to figure out how to limit what they did with their time, they struggled to figure out what to do with their time.

Today we have endless options, which is simultaneously wonderful and terrible, right? It's great having choices, but filling our days with all the things we *can* do crowds out time for the things we're *called* to do.

Your calendar may be full of things you can do—events you can attend, groups you can join, businesses you can start. But when you take a closer look at those calendar entries, are they really the things you should be doing—the things you're called to do?

One thing God has called me to is investing in the lives of foster children. So once I understood today's principle, I set the guardrail for my calendar that if I'm ever too busy for a foster child, I'm too busy. I refuse to let my life get so full that I don't have time for the race God has specifically marked out for me.

Is it time for you to set a guardrail like that for your calendar? What are you doing just because you can, not because you're called? I can promise you this: when you're running the race marked out specifically for you, there is unexplainable joy and fulfillment.

JOURNAL YOUR THOUGHTS

....

....

....

....

....

CAN DO VS. CALLED TO

Open your calendar and place every activity from this week into one of the two columns below.

If you get stuck, remember that things you're called to are roles and passions that are unique to you.

THINGS I CAN DO

THINGS I'M CALLED TO

Cooking class with a friend

Taking Mom to the doctor

What is one activity from the **Things I Can Do** column that you could take a break from (or stop doing entirely) in order to create breathing room?

....

What is one activity from the **Things I'm Called To** column that would be your own version of the filter, *"If I'm ever too busy for a foster child, then I'm too busy"*?

....

IF I'M EVER TOO BUSY TO

_____ ,

THEN I'M TOO BUSY.

> BE VERY CAREFUL, THEN, HOW YOU LIVE—
> NOT AS UNWISE BUT AS WISE, MAKING THE MOST
> OF EVERY OPPORTUNITY, BECAUSE THE DAYS
> ARE EVIL. THEREFORE DO NOT BE FOOLISH, BUT
> UNDERSTAND WHAT THE LORD'S WILL IS.
>
> *Ephesians 5:15–17*

Every May, my parents rent a beach house on Hilton Head Island for a big family vacation. The water is still a little chilly in late May, but not too chilly for the younger grandchildren. They grab surfboards and floats and jump right in. Within a matter of minutes, the current has taken them yards down the beach. But the drift is so gentle, they don't even notice. Only the parents waving like maniacs from the shore remind them to walk back up the beach to safety.

This isn't just a beach phenomenon though, is it? It happens in life too. When we stop paying attention, we drift. And the forces on our time will always pull us toward more, not margin.

So just like us adults waving the kids back up the beach to safety, we would be wise to recognize the signs that our calendars are drifting toward danger.

In his letter to the Ephesians, the apostle Paul offers a warning: "Be careful how you walk." He was aware that when we lift our feet and allow the current of society to carry us, we drift in negative directions. Before we know it, we are treading in the dangerous waters of exhaustion, overcommitment, and short-temperedness.

What does it look like when you've drifted too far—when you've squeezed all the breathing room out of your schedule? Are there some warning signs that can help you identify the "calendar drift" before it leads to those dangerous waters? Spend some time really answering those questions today. Learning to say no before your calendar is out of control is far less painful than having to back out or tough your way through too many obligations. Let's be careful how we walk and avoid that dangerous drift.

JOURNAL YOUR THOUGHTS

....

....

....

....

....

....

....

....

SPY ON YOUR TIME

We all enjoy mindless distractions every now and then. But left unchecked, our distractions can consume what little breathing room we have.

Take a minute to identify a few ways you might inadvertently be misusing your time.

☐ Social media   ☐ Email

☐ Binging on television   ☐ Gossip magazines

☐ Digital games   ☐ ....

☐ Taking, editing, posting photos   ☐ ....

☐ Online shopping   ☐ ....

How much time have you spent on these pastimes in the last 24 hours? Be honest.

....

....

....

Think back to the last time you were frazzled from too much going on. Which of these do you find yourself doing when your calendar is short on breathing room?

☐ Driving too fast

☐ Crying

☐ Yelling, "Hurry up!"

☐ Missing important events

☐ Losing your patience with loved ones

☐ Being unable to get started on anything

☐ Avoiding or snapping at people

☐ ....

☐ ....

☐ ....

What can you use as a warning sign that your calendar has drifted and is getting too full? Consider the things you just marked above.

I'll know I need to make breathing room when I find myself avoiding my mom's phone calls.

....

....

....

....

....

59

> THE PRUDENT SEE DANGER AND TAKE REFUGE,
> BUT THE SIMPLE KEEP GOING AND PAY THE PENALTY.
>
> *Proverbs 27:12*

My husband, Andy, and I have been praying this verse for as long as I can remember. We began praying it early in our marriage. We taught our children to pray it. We pray it for ourselves, for our kids, and for our church.

Heavenly Father, give us the wisdom to see trouble coming before it gets here and the courage to do something about it no matter what people think.

We've seen God answer this prayer in amazing ways over the years, especially as it relates to keeping breathing room in our schedules. At times it's taken courage, as other people wondered what in the world we were doing declining opportunities that from the outside looked too good to pass up.

But this prayer is a framework that makes decisions about how we spend our time so much easier. Will saying yes to something today cause trouble down the road? Then we should "take refuge." Maybe that means removing something else from our schedule. Maybe it means asking friends or family for help. Or maybe it means saying no for now.

Yesterday we looked at time's drift toward more, not margin. I encourage you to use today's verse as your prayer the moment you recognize you're running out of breathing room. Or better yet, use it to ask God to help you avoid the drift altogether. You'll be amazed at God's faithfulness to give you eyes to see trouble lurking just a few months ahead on your calendar.

JOURNAL YOUR THOUGHTS

....

....

....

....

....

....

....

....

....

....

MORE OR LESS

If you could ADD anything to your schedule, what would it be?

Examples: a night at home, more free time to paint

....

....

....

Are any of the fears we've talked about keeping you from making time for these things? Journal your thoughts.

☐ Fear of Missing Out
☐ Fear of Not Mattering
☐ Fear of Falling Behind
☐ Fear of Disappointing Others

....

....

....

....

....

If you could REMOVE anything from your schedule, what would it be?

Examples: a volunteer position, weekend business trips

....

....

....

Are any of the fears we've talked about keeping you from giving up these obligations? Journal your thoughts.

☐ Fear of Missing Out
☐ Fear of Not Mattering
☐ Fear of Falling Behind
☐ Fear of Disappointing Others

....

....

....

....

....

AND I TELL YOU THAT YOU ARE PETER, AND ON THIS ROCK I WILL BUILD MY CHURCH, AND THE GATES OF HADES WILL NOT OVERCOME IT.

Matthew 16:18

ALL THE DAYS ORDAINED FOR ME WERE WRITTEN IN YOUR BOOK BEFORE ONE OF THEM CAME TO BE.

Psalm 139:16

Time, from God's perspective, is completely different than time from our perspective. The cool thing is that God doesn't just see our past and our present. He has a complete view of our future too.

This is great news for us. When God looks at us, he doesn't just see us as we are in the moment. He sees our full potential, our whole timeline at once. God doesn't just shake his head in frustration over our current poor choices or missed opportunities. He actually sees what's next and next and next.

We read an example of this in the way Jesus perceived Peter. Impulsive, sometimes unstable, speak-before-you-think Peter seemed to be one of Jesus' favorites. His given name was Simon, but since Jesus saw Simon's future, he knew his potential. Matthew 16 records the conversation where Jesus changed Simon's name to Peter, meaning "rock." Jesus knew that Peter would ultimately be strong, courageous, and influential.

One of my all-time favorite Bible passages is Psalm 139. Something about verse 16 overwhelms me every time I read it. *"All the days ordained for me were written in your book before one of them came to be."* He's not writing our stories as we go, surprised by our choices and caught off-guard by our decisions. Every day ordained for me is already written in his book. He knows me and loves me anyway. He knew Peter and loved him anyway. He knows **you** and loves you anyway.

So as you persevere in changing how you view your time, take a deep breath and cut yourself a little slack. Creating breathing room is a long game of getting your priorities in order. That may require patience as you untangle from obligations. But God already sees the future you're moving toward and he will wait patiently. You can exhale.

JOURNAL YOUR THOUGHTS

....

....

....

....

....

....

....

....

LOOKING BACK, MOVING FORWARD

We can often find the motivation to make (or continue making) a change by looking back at how far we've already come.

Write down three words that described you 10 years ago.

_____   _____   _____

Circle which ones, if any, still describe you today.

What activities took up most of your time 10 years ago?

_____   _____   _____

Circle which ones, if any, you still spend time doing today.

What is one thing you've accomplished, one habit you've changed, or one milestone you've met that your younger self would never have believed you could do?

> VERY EARLY IN THE MORNING, WHILE IT WAS STILL
> DARK, JESUS GOT UP, LEFT THE HOUSE AND WENT
> OFF TO A SOLITARY PLACE, WHERE HE PRAYED.
>
> *Mark 1:35*

I need to let you in on a little secret. I'm a preacher's wife, an occasional Bible teacher, a person who loves Jesus intensely—and I have to admit that when my margin runs thin, my time alone with God suffers first. I know it's the last thing I should let slip. There are plenty of other things that could be and should be on the chopping block. And yet, my time with God is often the first thing to go.

Is the same thing true for you? Maybe we do this because other things feel more urgent. But the truth is, nothing is more important, even more urgent, than our intimacy with God. From our intimacy with God flows the health and well-being of all our other relationships. From our intimacy with God flows the rhythm of life that allows for the breathing room we desperately need.

We get a pretty clear message from Jesus in the way he modeled time alone with God. All four Gospels record Jesus stealing away to spend time alone in prayer.

Interestingly, most of the examples recorded come right on the heels of significant ministry success, when the demand for his time and attention would have been highest. It seems that

Jesus did exactly the opposite of what I'm tempted to do. In busy seasons, he refused to let his time with God become optional.

Is that as convicting for you as it is for me? Let's reorient our priorities so we have the breathing room in our days—especially in our busiest seasons—for the one thing that's most important.

JOURNAL YOUR THOUGHTS

....

....

....

....

....

....

....

....

....

....

....

....

FINDING QUIET TIME

Traditionally, when we think of quiet time, we think of reading the Bible alone in the early morning hours—before coffee, kids, and the day's chaos begins. For some seasons of life, that can be unrealistic.

Let's think outside the box. Check any of the ideas on these pages that would fit well into your life, or write down any others that come to mind.

What piece of your day could you set aside for quiet time?

☐ Before you go to bed

☐ Your lunch hour

☐ Your child's nap time

☐ Mid-morning or afternoon "tea time"

☐ ....

What are some activities that could enhance your quiet time?

☐ Listening to a sermon

☐ Reading a devotion on your phone

☐ Playing worship music

☐ Listening to your Bible app read to you

☐ ....

How could you create accountability for making your quiet time a priority?

☐ Share your plans with your family.

☐ Block off the time each day on your calendar.

☐ Set an alarm or reminder on your phone.

☐ Find a friend to be an accountability and encouragement partner.

☐ ....

DO YOU NOT KNOW? HAVE YOU NOT HEARD? THE LORD IS THE EVERLASTING GOD, THE CREATOR OF THE ENDS OF THE EARTH. HE WILL NOT GROW TIRED OR WEARY, AND HIS UNDERSTANDING NO ONE CAN FATHOM.

HE GIVES STRENGTH TO THE WEARY AND INCREASES THE POWER OF THE WEAK. EVEN YOUTHS GROW TIRED AND WEARY, AND YOUNG MEN STUMBLE AND FALL; BUT THOSE WHO HOPE IN THE LORD WILL RENEW THEIR STRENGTH. THEY WILL SOAR ON WINGS LIKE EAGLES; THEY WILL RUN AND NOT GROW WEARY, THEY WILL WALK AND NOT BE FAINT.

Isaiah 40:28–31

I think there's a difference between being tired and being weary. To me, being tired is your body needing to rest at the end of a productive day. Weary is that thing you feel all the way to your bones. It's physical exhaustion combined with the emotional exhaustion of being anxious or overwhelmed or sad.

Sometimes the things that make us weary also make it impossible to create breathing room in our schedules. A health crisis, the demands of caring for an aging parent, even particularly intense seasons of motherhood can make you weary. And creating margin isn't always possible with doctor appointments to attend or a new baby to care for.

If you don't have a circumstance making you weary right now, you will eventually—we all will. So I want to wrap up our look at creating breathing room in our time with a bit of encouragement for those seasons when making margin in our schedules simply isn't possible.

Today's reading has a promise for us to cling to on our most wearisome days. Isaiah tells us that when we "hope in the Lord"—when we read God's Word and trust God's will—he will renew our strength. Maybe that will look like dinner delivered by a friend. Or maybe it will be clarity on what to drop from your "to-do" list for now. Be assured, though, that God will meet you when your margin runs out.

And, eventually, the season will pass. So let's honor God by living with breathing room when we can… and by hoping in him when we can't.

JOURNAL YOUR THOUGHTS

....

....

....

....

....

....

....

HOPE FOR THE WEARY

If you're running on fumes with no end in sight, remember that the Lord will renew your strength. Let's cling to that promise today.

What is currently making you (or has recently made you) weary?

....

....

....

....

....

In the past, what are some ways God has renewed you when you were weary?

☐ Dinner delivered by a friend

☐ A good, hearty laugh

☐ A good, hearty cry

☐ Note of encouragement delivered by surprise

☐ A well-timed invitation or cancellation

☐ ....

Complete this prayer with your own words.

Father, thank you for the promise that you will meet me where I am and give me strength when I need it. I am so grateful for all the ways you provide for me in my weariness and for the people you put in my life when I need them the most. I pray for endurance in this season and that I will continue this journey with a joyful, appreciative heart.

....

....

....

....

....

....

....

....

....

....

....

....

....

....

MONEY

3

Bottom Line:

Your money's direction shows your heart's affection.

YOUR MONEY'S DIRECTION
shows your heart's affection.

....

....

....

....

....

....

....

....

....

....

....

....

....

....

1 | Are you naturally a spender or a saver?

2 | What example did your parents set for you in how they handled their finances?

3 | Share an example of a time you or someone you know "traded your peace for a purchase."

4 | Which of the four fears most often tempts you to spend money you shouldn't? Why is that?

☐ Fear of Missing Out
☐ Fear of Not Mattering
☐ Fear of Falling Behind
☐ Fear of Disappointing Others

5 | In Luke 16:13, Jesus says, "You cannot serve both God and money." Sandra shared a few examples of this dilemma, like feeling called to leave your job but not having the financial stability to do so. Can you think of a time when you've faced a similar situation?

NOTES

....

....

....

....

....

....

....

....

....

....

....

....

....

....

....

....

FOR WE BROUGHT NOTHING INTO THE WORLD,
AND WE CAN TAKE NOTHING OUT OF IT.

1 Timothy 6:7

MOREOVER, WHEN GOD GIVES SOMEONE WEALTH
AND POSSESSIONS, AND THE ABILITY TO ENJOY
THEM, TO ACCEPT THEIR LOT AND BE HAPPY
IN THEIR TOIL—THIS IS A GIFT OF GOD.

Ecclesiastes 5:19

The verbs we use when talking about money make the truth we find in today's verses a little harder to remember. We usually say that you *earn* money, *make* money, or sometimes *invest* money. But *steward* money? You don't hear that very often.

The typical attitude toward money is that you own what you earn. I mean, it feels like I own my money and the stuff I've bought with it. I'm the one who has put in the hard work and made the wise investments.

But the truth is that what I consider *mine* doesn't belong to me. I have no permanent claim on the dollars in my bank account or even the home where I lay my head at night.

You don't even have to believe in Jesus for this to be true. What Paul wrote to his friend Timothy in today's verse is not specifically a Christian truth. It's just a human truth. Our money existed before it was ours, and it will be someone else's after we die.

To start this week's look at creating breathing room in our finances, we have to begin by acknowledging that we are not owners; we are simply stewards—temporary managers—of our earthly wealth and possessions. And if we believe that God is the ultimate owner, then we should manage our money the way he asks us to.

JOURNAL YOUR THOUGHTS

....

....

....

....

....

....

....

....

....

....

DEBT OR DISCIPLINE

In this week's video, Sandra said, "You can raise your standard of living with debt. You can only raise your quality of life with discipline." Have you ever stopped to think about the difference between those two?

God cares more about your quality of life

THAN YOUR STANDARD OF LIVING.

....

....

....

....

....

....

What are some things that tempt you to prioritize your standard of living, maybe even with debt?

Examples: a renovated kitchen, lots of Christmas presents for the kids

....

....

....

What is something that would increase your current quality of life?

Example: a weekend away with my spouse

....

....

....

What disciplined action(s) do you need to take to achieve that?

Example: Cut down the number of times we eat out each week and put the savings in our travel fund.

....

....

....

THEN HE SAID TO THEM, "WATCH OUT! BE ON YOUR GUARD AGAINST ALL KINDS OF GREED; LIFE DOES NOT CONSIST IN AN ABUNDANCE OF POSSESSIONS."

AND HE TOLD THEM THIS PARABLE: "THE GROUND OF A CERTAIN RICH MAN YIELDED AN ABUNDANT HARVEST. HE THOUGHT TO HIMSELF, 'WHAT SHALL I DO? I HAVE NO PLACE TO STORE MY CROPS.' THEN HE SAID, 'THIS IS WHAT I'LL DO. I WILL TEAR DOWN MY BARNS AND BUILD BIGGER ONES, AND THERE I WILL STORE MY SURPLUS GRAIN.' AND I'LL SAY TO MYSELF, 'YOU HAVE PLENTY OF GRAIN LAID UP FOR MANY YEARS. TAKE LIFE EASY; EAT, DRINK AND BE MERRY.' BUT GOD SAID TO HIM, 'YOU FOOL! THIS VERY NIGHT YOUR LIFE WILL BE DEMANDED FROM YOU. THEN WHO WILL GET WHAT YOU HAVE PREPARED FOR YOURSELF?' THIS IS HOW IT WILL BE WITH WHOEVER STORES UP THINGS FOR THEMSELVES BUT IS NOT RICH TOWARD GOD."

Luke 12:15–21

One day as Jesus was teaching a huge crowd, an argument broke out. One brother accused another of being greedy and not sharing his inheritance. Because Jesus was the master of seizing teachable moments, he decided to use a parable to communicate a lesson on greed.

He lays the groundwork for his point by telling the story of a rich man who had an incredible harvest. But the rich man ran into a little problem. His crop was so plentiful that he didn't have room to store it all. So he solved his problem by building bigger barns, choosing to stockpile rather than share. That taken care of, he patted himself on the back and planned to kick back, relax, and enjoy luxurious living. It didn't end well.

The farmer in Jesus' parable made the same mistake you and I are likely to make when it comes to having more than we need—we *assume* we should *consume* it all.

Here's something I know about you: you live on a percentage of your income. And if you haven't stopped to pick one, culture has picked one for you—maybe even convincing you to spend beyond 100 percent of what's coming in. But in today's parable, God refutes the assumption that it's all for our consumption. We're not supposed to just spend and save; we're supposed to *steward*.

Having financial breathing room means living on a percentage of your income that leaves you with some surplus. This creates an opportunity to partner with—or "be rich toward"— God... but only if you're willing to limit your lifestyle and embrace the idea that life consists of far more than the abundance of our possessions. How awesome to begin thinking now about how to maximize the potential of our extra for God's kingdom, not ours. That's the very best kind of *breathing room*.

PERCENTAGE LIVE-ER

Perhaps you've heard of being a "percentage giver"—committing to share a specific percentage of your income rather than a fixed dollar amount. What about also being a "percentage live-er"?

Let's start by looking at how you're currently spending your money. Write down the percentage of your income that currently goes to each of these three categories.

Money I **live on**   .... %
(e.g., housing, auto, food)

Money I **save**   + ... %
(e.g., retirement accounts, investments)

Money I **give away**   + ... %
(e.g., tithe, charitable giving)

                               = **100%**

Divide this pie chart into **Give**, **Save**, and **Live** sections according to the percentages you just calculated.

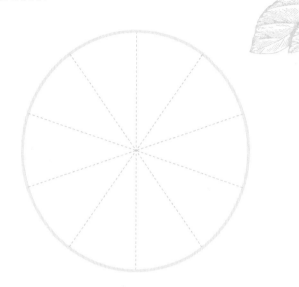

What are your thoughts and feelings as you look at your completed chart? What if you were showing it to someone else?

....

....

....

The **save** and **give** pieces of your financial pie are where you find breathing room. So, what changes, if any, would you like to make to the way you allocate your money?

....

....

....

> SELL YOUR POSSESSIONS AND GIVE TO THE POOR. PROVIDE PURSES FOR YOURSELVES THAT WILL NOT WEAR OUT, A TREASURE IN HEAVEN THAT WILL NEVER FAIL, WHERE NO THIEF COMES NEAR AND NO MOTH DESTROYS. FOR WHERE YOUR TREASURE IS, THERE YOUR HEART WILL BE ALSO.
>
> *Luke 12:33–34*

The snippet of Jesus' teaching we're looking at today comes at the end of a much longer speech—one you've likely heard before. In it, Jesus illustrates for his disciples that they can trust God because he provides so well even for the birds and the wildflowers. *"And how much more valuable you are than birds!"* he tells them in Luke 12:24.

This is such a reassuring truth to consider before we start making the tough decisions required to keep breathing room in our finances. You are a beloved daughter of God. You can trust him to provide everything you need.

If you're naturally a saver, you may be inclined to keep a tight fist on your money, refusing to be generous because you're trusting in your bank account to provide. If you're naturally a spender, you may be buying your way to a feeling of safety, trusting in your stored-up stuff.

God is asking you to trust him, and money is a tool for doing that.

The end of today's verse explains it so clearly. Your money's direction shows your heart's affection. How you handle your finances shines a bright light on the condition of your heart.

So how's your heart? What does your checkbook say about where you're placing your trust? If someone peeked over your shoulder at your credit card statement, would they see you following God's urging to be generous? One way to check the condition of your heart may just be checking your receipts.

JOURNAL YOUR THOUGHTS

....

....

....

....

....

....

....

....

....

....

....

JUSTIFYING EXPENSES

So, let's say someone actually could see into your financial accounts. What are you spending money on that's not in your budget? For some, it may be treating a friend to coffee or pitching in to help a co-worker in need. For others, it's that unplanned but "needed" dress or the expensive photographer fee for cool family photos like all your friends have.

It's real. We all feel it. Here's a challenge for you.

Look at last month's credit card or bank statement. Which expenses would you have a hard time justifying to someone else? Jot them down in the space provided.

....

....

....

....

....

....

....

As you look at the items you've just listed, how do you feel?

☐ Disappointed   ☐ Happy   ☐ Stressed

☐ Disapproving   ☐ Embarrassed   ☐ Anxious

☐ Proud   ☐ Remorseful   ☐ Overwhelmed

☐ Guilty   ☐ Ashamed   ☐ Confused

☐ Let down   ☐ Amazed   ☐ Frustrated

☐ Content   ☐ Satisfied   ☐ Thrilled

☐ Annoyed   ☐ Surprised   ☐ ....

This week's video said, "Money is the most powerful tool we'll ever have for learning to trust our heavenly Father." Does this match how you were first taught to think about money? Is it how you view money now? Journal your thoughts.

....

....

....

....

....

....

....

COMMAND THOSE WHO ARE RICH IN THIS PRESENT WORLD NOT TO BE ARROGANT NOR TO PUT THEIR HOPE IN WEALTH, WHICH IS SO UNCERTAIN, BUT TO PUT THEIR HOPE IN GOD, WHO RICHLY PROVIDES US WITH EVERYTHING FOR OUR ENJOYMENT. COMMAND THEM TO DO GOOD, TO BE RICH IN GOOD DEEDS, AND TO BE GENEROUS AND WILLING TO SHARE. IN THIS WAY THEY WILL LAY UP TREASURE FOR THEMSELVES AS A FIRM FOUNDATION FOR THE COMING AGE, SO THAT THEY MAY TAKE HOLD OF THE LIFE THAT IS TRULY LIFE.

1 Timothy 6:17–19

Recently I got a panicked call from my 17-year-old foster daughter. She was on the side of the highway with a blown-out tire. The ground on the shoulder of the road was too wet for the jack to work, so we were going to need a tow truck. While waiting two and a half hours for help to arrive, with my patience dwindling by the minute, I realized I was in the middle of a "rich person problem."

What is a "rich person problem"? It's a term that's become pretty popular around our house and in our churches. (First, a note: You may not *feel rich* compared to your friends or neighbors, but zoom out a bit and consider how you might stack up globally. Having a roof over your head and food at every meal means you are indeed rich.) Rich person problems have to do with things like computer issues, car trouble, flight delays, missed deliveries, not making the sale, not getting the bonus, late tow trucks, etc. They aren't life-threatening, but they are annoying and inconvenient. And we tend to get pretty bent out of shape over them.

In the heat of the moment, it's easy for us to confuse rich person problems with real problems. We spend money to make ourselves comfortable, and when the bumps and bruises come, we get angry. We take our eyes off of our heavenly Father and place our hope in things that don't deliver. We become dependent on earthly treasures and forget their disappointing and temporary nature. But as Paul tells us in today's verse, when we put our hope in God, when we keep an eternal perspective and let our actions follow, we can take hold of "the life that is truly life."

JOURNAL YOUR THOUGHTS

....

....

....

....

....

....

....

....

A NEW WAY TO BE RICH

What's the last rich person problem you lost your cool over?
How do you feel about it in hindsight?

....

....

....

....

....

....

....

....

....

....

....

....

In today's verse, Paul gives us the formula for avoiding rich person problems. He tells us "to do good, to be rich in good deeds, and to be generous and willing to share."

Write down one practical way you could do each of those things this week.

- "Do good"
  Example: Offer a sincere compliment to the coffee shop guy who's not very friendly

- "Be rich in good deeds"
  Example: Deliver cookies to the family who just moved to the neighborhood

- "Be generous and willing to share"
  Example: Watch a friend's kids so she doesn't have to pay a babysitter

> WHOEVER LOVES MONEY NEVER HAS MONEY ENOUGH;
> WHOEVER LOVES WEALTH IS NEVER SATISFIED
> WITH HIS INCOME. THIS TOO IS MEANINGLESS.
>
> *Ecclesiastes 5:10*

Depending on how you're wired, the idea of limiting your spending in order to create financial breathing room may feel restrictive, like you're being fenced in. But if you're a dog owner like me, you know that fences are about *creating* freedom, not limiting it. A backyard fence allows our dog to be outside longer and off-leash more. The fence is a way to give her more freedom, not less.

The boundary of breathing room in your finances works exactly the same way. It allows you to say yes to God's great plans for your life without having to wait until your credit score has improved. It's about having *more* freedom to follow Christ.

If God calls you to move to a new city or take a new job, don't you want to be able to say yes? If he nudges you to donate to a cause or respond generously to a need, wouldn't it be great to be able to? These are the actions that will improve your quality of life. But your ability to follow Christ depends on your willingness to get your financial house in order.

As today's verse reminds us, money will never satisfy. There's nothing you can buy, no standard of living that will make you as happy as living in line with God's plans for you. Waiting just on the other side of a decision to keep some margin in your finances is a *richly* fulfilling life—the very best kind of riches.

JOURNAL YOUR THOUGHTS

....

....

....

....

....

....

....

....

....

....

....

It's about having more freedom to follow Christ.

FINDING MARGIN SO YOU CAN SAY YES

Often we don't feel the weight of our financial messes until we bump up against an opportunity we wish we could say yes to.

What are some *big* dreams—or perhaps even callings—you'd love to pursue if money weren't an issue?

Examples: starting a business, adopting a child

....

....

....

....

What are some *smaller* ways you are saying yes to God with your finances?

Example: supporting a friend's mission trip

....

....

....

....

....

Is there anything you've had to say no to because you didn't have the financial margin?

....

....

....

....

....

....

....

....

....

....

....

....

....

....

> KEEP YOUR LIVES FREE FROM THE LOVE OF MONEY AND BE
> CONTENT WITH WHAT YOU HAVE, BECAUSE GOD HAS SAID,
> "NEVER WILL I LEAVE YOU; NEVER WILL I FORSAKE YOU."
>
> *Hebrews 13:5*

Think about all the times you pulled out your wallet in the last week. You probably paid for groceries, maybe put gas in your car. Perhaps you paid the babysitter. These are "fixed expenses," the costs you encounter every week just to keep your life running smoothly. Could you trim a bit from these costs to create some financial breathing room? Probably.

But there is another category of expenses that I think God is more interested in addressing than how much you spend on cereal and sandwich supplies. Instead of "fixed expenses," we'll call them "fear expenses." This is the money you spend out of insecurity or anxiety—the car you leased, the trip you took, the home you bought… When motivated by pleasing or keeping up with others, these are "fear expenses." And they are often big-ticket items that you may be making payments on for years to come.

When insecurity and fear drive our spending, we end up in a mess every single time. But the author of Hebrews offers an alternative: contentment instead of comparison and trust in a God who says, *"Never will I forsake you."* For the Hebrew people, this was a reminder of a promise that dated back centuries—*fear not, God is with you.* We need this reminder today just as much as they did.

You can release the fear that *you'll be the only one without* or that *she'll be so disappointed.* God's not going to leave you stranded. He can change hearts and restore relationships. To find breathing room in your finances, identify the fear and choose to trust God instead.

JOURNAL YOUR THOUGHTS

....

....

....

....

....

....

....

....

....

....

....

....

FIXED EXPENSES VS. FEAR EXPENSES

Below is a list of common expenses. For those that apply to you, sort them into one of the two columns, fixed expenses or fear expenses. *(Remember, your filter for identifying fear expenses is whether you took on the expense just to please or keep up with others.)*

Groceries	Health & Beauty	Rent/Mortgage	Entertainment
Car Payment	Student Loan	Clothing	Home/Car Repairs
Dining Out	Utilities	Home Furnishings	Wedding
Vacations	Insurance	Medical Bills	Kids' Activities

Take some additional time to add your own expenses—even the ones you'd rather forget.

FIXED EXPENSES   FEAR EXPENSES

....

....

....

....

....

....

Which of the fears we've talked about influence the way you spend your money? Journal your thoughts.

☐ Fear of Missing Out
☐ Fear of Not Mattering
☐ Fear of Falling Behind
☐ Fear of Disappointing Others

....

....

....

....

....

What burdens—financial or otherwise—would it be nice to hand over to God?

....

....

....

....

....

....

> "COME TO ME, ALL YOU WHO ARE WEARY AND BURDENED,
> AND I WILL GIVE YOU REST. TAKE MY YOKE UPON YOU
> AND LEARN FROM ME, FOR I AM GENTLE AND HUMBLE
> IN HEART, AND YOU WILL FIND REST FOR YOUR SOULS.
> FOR MY YOKE IS EASY AND MY BURDEN IS LIGHT."
>
> *Matthew 11:28–30*

If I can get away with not checking bags when I fly, I do. There's something about hopping off a plane, bag in hand, and heading straight for the exit that makes me feel efficient and productive. I *really* like efficient and productive.

On a recent trip, my bag was stuffed beyond full, but I had committed to packing a carry-on suitcase. I wrestled it out of the overhead bin and bumped every seat as I made my way off the plane. At the end of the jetway, I realized I was at the farthest terminal from the airport exit doors. That meant a long walk plus train rides. By the time I made it outside, my back hurt and my legs hurt and my arms hurt and my feelings hurt. And it was my own fault.

A financial mistake can be a heavy burden too—one that you may have to carry for years. You may be *wishing* you could create breathing room in your personal finances, but you're still paying the price for an ill-advised loan, a bad investment, or a few late payments. Or maybe money has tainted your relationship with your parents, your spouse, or your kids.

If you are weary from the long, hard work of cleaning up a financial mess—your own or someone else's—Jesus simply says, *"Come to me."* He's waiting to bear your burdens for you, and he will make a trade. You can hand over your heavy suitcase of troubles, worries, fears, and anxieties. And he will give you emotional breathing room even if it may be a long time before you can find it in your finances.

JOURNAL YOUR THOUGHTS

....

....

....

....

....

....

....

....

....

....

....

....

SCRIPTURE TO KEEP YOU ON TRACK

Draw or journal your thoughts about the following passage. Use it as a jumping-off point for a few minutes of prayer about God's role in your finances.

Consider memorizing this line: *"…give me neither poverty nor riches, but give me only my daily bread."* What a powerful way to declare that we trust not in our own riches, but in a God who richly provides.

TWO THINGS I ASK OF YOU, LORD;

DO NOT REFUSE ME BEFORE I DIE:

KEEP FALSEHOOD AND LIES FAR FROM ME;

GIVE ME NEITHER POVERTY NOR RICHES,

BUT GIVE ME ONLY MY DAILY BREAD.

OTHERWISE, I MAY HAVE TOO MUCH AND DISOWN YOU

AND SAY, "WHO IS THE LORD?"

OR I MAY BECOME POOR AND STEAL,

AND SO DISHONOR THE NAME OF MY GOD.

Proverbs 30:7-9

RELATIONSHIPS

> *Bottom Line:*
> Don't trade what's unique to you for something someone else can do.

DON'T TRADE WHAT'S UNIQUE
TO YOU FOR SOMETHING
SOMEONE ELSE CAN DO.

VIDEO REFLECTIONS

....

....

....

....

....

....

....

....

....

....

....

....

....

....

DISCUSSION QUESTIONS

1 | How did the video of the mother and daughter make you feel?

2 | Have you ever been on the other side of someone who didn't have time for you—someone with no breathing room? What was it like?

3 | Think about some of your unique roles (e.g., daughter, mom, wife, sister, aunt, best friend). Which of these relationships is currently getting your leftovers? How do you feel about that?

4 | Which of the four fears has caused you to take on *something someone else can do?*

  ☐ Fear of Missing Out
  ☐ Fear of Not Mattering
  ☐ Fear of Falling Behind
  ☐ Fear of Disappointing Others

5 | Nehemiah 6:3 says, "I am doing a great work and I cannot come down." What activities or opportunities are currently tempting you away from your unique roles—your "great work"?

NOTES

...AND YET I WILL SHOW YOU THE MOST EXCELLENT WAY. IF I SPEAK IN THE TONGUES OF MEN OR OF ANGELS, BUT DO NOT HAVE LOVE, I AM ONLY A RESOUNDING GONG OR A CLANGING CYMBAL. IF I HAVE THE GIFT OF PROPHECY AND CAN FATHOM ALL MYSTERIES AND ALL KNOWLEDGE, AND IF I HAVE A FAITH THAT CAN MOVE MOUNTAINS, BUT DO NOT HAVE LOVE, I AM NOTHING. IF I GIVE ALL I POSSESS TO THE POOR AND GIVE OVER MY BODY TO HARDSHIP THAT I MAY BOAST, BUT DO NOT HAVE LOVE, I GAIN NOTHING.

LOVE IS PATIENT, LOVE IS KIND. IT DOES NOT ENVY, IT DOES NOT BOAST, IT IS NOT PROUD. IT DOES NOT DISHONOR OTHERS, IT IS NOT SELF-SEEKING, IT IS NOT EASILY ANGERED, IT KEEPS NO RECORD OF WRONGS.

1 Corinthians 12:31–13:5

The last time I came to 1 Corinthians 13 when reading my Bible, I kind of wanted to skip it. I mean, good grief, I've read it or heard it ten thousand times! You probably have too. But the verse leading up to this famous passage caught my eye. Paul makes a pretty big promise: *"I will show you the most excellent way."* Not a really good way? Not even a great way, or an excellent way, but *the most excellent* way? It seems like we should probably pay attention!

What follows that eye-catching statement is a list of activities that are not "the most excellent way." And what Paul includes would have surprised his audience. His language may not be familiar in our cultural context, but to a first-century Christian, it would have sounded like a highlight reel of talents. Paul's speech would have left his audience feeling the same way that a scroll through social media can for you—everyone else is so much smarter, prettier, more talented…

Yet Paul says, *All those things you think are so impressive? None of them matter without love.*

God isn't impressed by our personal accomplishments. He is more interested in our relationships—in how well we love one another. The most excellent way to live, it turns out, is by being patient, kind, humble, and selfless toward others.

Living at your limit, running frantically from one obligation to the next, is not the best strategy for becoming patient, kind, or selfless. So if God's priority is for us to love one another, let's start by making some breathing room for the "one anothers" we love.

JOURNAL YOUR THOUGHTS

....

....

....

....

....

PRIORITIZING PEOPLE

Today's verse reminds us that the world's definition of success is not God's definition of success. Is it possible you're chasing the wrong one?

What is one activity or accomplishment you're really proud of?
Example: Successfully running my own side business

....

What is one benefit you enjoy from it?
Example: Extra income

....

What does it cost you?
Example: I only sleep four hours each night.

....

How does it impact your relationship with loved ones?
Example: I haven't had time to go out with friends in months.

....

IF GOD'S PRIORITY IS FOR US
TO LOVE ONE ANOTHER,
let's start by making some breathing room
FOR THE "ONE ANOTHERS" WE LOVE.

Are you pursuing God's priority of "loving one another"? Journal your thoughts.

....

....

....

....

....

....

....

> NOW ABOUT YOUR LOVE FOR ONE ANOTHER WE DO
> NOT NEED TO WRITE TO YOU, FOR YOU YOURSELVES
> HAVE BEEN TAUGHT BY GOD TO LOVE EACH OTHER.
>
> *1 Thessalonians 4:9*

It has always been hard to buy a shirt for my dad. Not because he's persnickety about style or fabrics or colors, but because he's always been picky about the size of the front pocket.

The front pocket—in Dad's pre-iPhone days—needed to be wide enough to hold his pen, his mechanical pencil, and his little spiral notebook. The notebook contained his kids' ever-changing phone numbers, our current class schedules, and later, our work schedules. He never kept that stuff close in order to check up on us. My dad, to this day, just makes sure he knows how to be engaged with and how to talk intelligently about what's important to the people who are important to him. He loves well with his time and his actions.

Right there in his notebook, he had what amounted to a written list of his *inner-circle* people—the folks to whom he was the one and only dad, husband, sibling, or son. Inner-circle people are those for whom you, and only you, can ever fill your role. Your boss can find another employee, but your parents can't find another daughter; your son can't find another mom.

So often, we unintentionally let *outer-circle* people get first dibs on our attention, leaving nothing but leftovers for the inner-circle spouse, parents, kids, and friends. That's why the first step in creating relational breathing room is to flip that around, figuring out who belongs permanently at the top of your priority list. Or, in my dad's case, in that trusty notebook close to his heart.

JOURNAL YOUR THOUGHTS

INNER-CIRCLE PEOPLE FIRST

Using the target, map the relationships in your life.

- **Inner Circle:** Which roles are unique to you?
  Examples: wife, sister, mother, daughter, aunt

- **Next Circle:** Which roles do you uniquely do, but you could still be replaced with some effort?
  Examples: employee, Bible study leader

- **Outer Circle:** In which roles are you easily replaceable?
  Examples: committee member, class participant

What's one thing you can do this week to prioritize the people in your innermost circle?

....

....

....

....

....

....

....

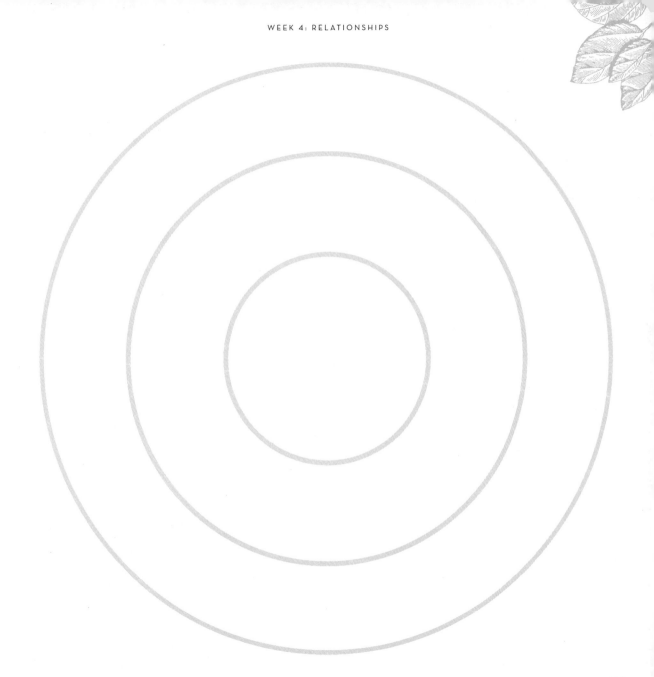

> SO I SENT MESSENGERS TO THEM, SAYING,
> "I AM DOING A GREAT WORK AND I CANNOT COME
> DOWN. WHY SHOULD THE WORK STOP WHILE
> I LEAVE IT AND COME DOWN TO YOU?"
>
> *Nehemiah 6:3 (NASB)*

Beth Holley was the quintessential southern lady. She passed away a few years ago, but because she was my sister's mother-in-law, I was lucky enough to know her. She always had a ready smile and a word of encouragement. In fact, it's a word—or a phrase, really—that I remember most about her.

Beth didn't drive much in her later years, but that didn't stop her from being on the go, thanks to her trademark phrase. When any of her children or grandchildren invited her to go somewhere, her response was immediate: "I'll be ready!" She didn't say, "Well, now, let me check the calendar." Or, "I suppose I can move some things around." She simply said to the people she loved so much, "I'll be ready!"

I don't know about you, but that inspires me to pieces! I want to be like Beth.

Do you know why Beth responded that way? She knew that time spent with her kids and grandkids was her "great work." She was a busy lady with lots of activities and options, but she didn't let them trump the most important people in her life.

Ladies, sometimes a simple *no* or *not right now* to someone in our outer circle can have a huge impact on someone in our inner circle. Nehemiah's statement in today's verse is a first-century way of saying, "Thanks for asking, but no, I'm not available." Let's practice politely declining invitations so we have enough margin in our time, energy, and attention to be able to say to our loved ones without hesitation, just like Beth, "I'll be ready!"

JOURNAL YOUR THOUGHTS

....

....

....

....

....

....

....

....

....

....

....

....

PRACTICING YES, PRACTICING NO

Wouldn't it be great to have a phrase like Beth's that tells your loved ones you'll always prioritize them first? Here are a few options. Feel free to write your own below.

- *Just tell me when!*

- *If you'll be there, I'll be there.*

- *You come first for me.*

- *I love any chance to spend time with you.*

- *I'll always make time for you.*

- ....

- ....

- ....

To be available to say yes to our inner-circle people, we may have to say no to invitations from others. Let's come up with a couple of polite ways to decline offers that would pull us away from the most important people in our lives.

Choose one of the phrases below (or write one for yourself) and practice saying it out loud (I know, it may feel silly). Keep the phrase handy next time you need to protect your breathing room.

- *Thank you for inviting me, but I'm not available.*

- *I'm flattered to be asked, but I can't commit right now.*

- *Sorry, I can't. Can I get a raincheck?*

- *I wouldn't be able to give you my best.*

- *I'm not taking on anything new right now.*

- ....

- ....

- ....

> DO NOTHING OUT OF SELFISH AMBITION
> OR VAIN CONCEIT. RATHER, IN HUMILITY VALUE
> OTHERS ABOVE YOURSELVES, NOT LOOKING
> TO YOUR OWN INTERESTS BUT EACH OF YOU
> TO THE INTERESTS OF THE OTHERS.
>
> *Philippians 2:3–4*

A few years ago, on the Friday before Labor Day, I was at the bank drive-thru making a deposit—one of a bunch of errands I was trying to accomplish before the long holiday weekend. As we wrapped up the transaction, I heard the teller say, "Remember. Wear clothes on Monday."

"Excuse me?" I responded to him (yes, HIM). "Wear clothes on Monday?"

"No ma'am, *WE'RE CLOSED* on Monday."

Oh my goodness. I immediately put my sunglasses back on, drove away, and determined it was time to find a new bank!

My point in sharing this story, other than to give you a chuckle at my expense, is that *not hearing* people is one of the most obvious symptoms that we've run out of breathing room. Multi-tasking through every chat and interaction is a sure sign that our priorities are out of order.

Listening is tough for me. I am a "to-do" list kind of girl. Interestingly, "listening" never makes it on the list. If I'm being completely honest, listening actually infringes on accomplishing the list. But I've learned that my list is far less important than my loved ones. And in order to really love them, *I must stop* what I'm doing and listen. It communicates: *You are more important to me than a computer screen, a cell phone, or a "to-do" list. You are more important to me than a meeting, an event, or anything else that might vie for my time. You are more important to me than anybody or anything else in my world.*

So what do you need to turn off or turn away from to really tune into your loved ones today? Doing so will bring breathing room back to your relationships. I promise.

JOURNAL YOUR THOUGHTS

ARE YOU LISTENING, REALLY?

Think back to a few scenarios where multitasking prevented you from being fully present for your inner-circle people. Write down a few of those situations below.

Examples: Talking on the phone while driving the kids to school, interrupting dinner to take a work call

....

....

....

....

....

....

....

....

....

....

Are there boundaries you can set up to prevent the tug of distraction? Write down a few possible guardrails below. Then circle one you can commit to right now.

Examples: No phone with passengers in the car, work can wait when I'm away from the office

....

....

....

....

....

....

....

....

....

....

A NEW COMMAND I GIVE YOU: LOVE ONE ANOTHER. AS I HAVE LOVED YOU, SO YOU MUST LOVE ONE ANOTHER. BY THIS ALL MEN WILL KNOW THAT YOU ARE MY DISCIPLES, IF YOU LOVE ONE ANOTHER.

John 13:34–35

A few years ago, Andy and I got a letter from a stranger. That's not such an unusual thing when you're a pastor and a pastor's wife, but this one made an unforgettable impression on us.

The letter began with a sad but not uncommon story of a marriage that started out strong but slowly began deteriorating with this young husband's longer and longer hours at work. He confessed that he had begun enjoying his work environment more than his home environment and had slowly begun inappropriately enjoying the company of a female co-worker.

During one late evening at the office, he and the co-worker decided to quickly grab dinner. As he looked up from his menu, he saw Andy and me sitting at a nearby booth. He said that we were talking and laughing about something, and in that moment, he was overwhelmed with the thought that he should be, and wanted to be, sitting in that restaurant talking and laughing with his wife.

It was a wake-up call that was almost, but not quite, too late. He went straight home and reordered his priorities so that the people he *most* loved would actually be *most* important.

Now, of course, reading that story made Andy and me grateful for even a small role in this man's changed direction. But there was also a lesson for us.

Sometimes we accidentally prioritize outer-circle people out of fear that we'll be judged for choosing to prioritize our families. "I can't because I'm having dinner with my husband" doesn't feel like a worthy enough excuse. But getting a letter that celebrated our decision to prioritize time with each other was a reminder that our commitment to our loved ones could be just the permission someone else needs to prioritize theirs.

After all, today's passage reminds us that loving each other well will make us stand out from the crowd. Or at least get noticed in the restaurant.

JOURNAL YOUR THOUGHTS

....

....

....

....

....

....

....

....

TRICKED BY FEAR

Can you think of a scenario where you prioritized outer-circle people over those in your inner circle?

....

....

....

....

....

....

....

....

....

....

Can you go one step further and label the fear that drove your decision? Write down what you were afraid would happen if you said no.

- Fear of Missing Out

- Fear of Not Mattering

- Fear of Falling Behind

- Fear of Disappointing Others

....

....

....

....

....

What would you do differently, if anything, if you were faced with the same scenario again?

....

....

....

....

....

> THEREFORE, IF YOU ARE OFFERING YOUR GIFT AT THE ALTAR AND THERE REMEMBER THAT YOUR BROTHER OR SISTER HAS SOMETHING AGAINST YOU, LEAVE YOUR GIFT THERE IN FRONT OF THE ALTAR. FIRST GO AND BE RECONCILED TO THEM; THEN COME AND OFFER YOUR GIFT.
>
> *Matthew 5:23–24*

Today's Scripture passage from the Sermon on the Mount surely surprised the men and women who heard Jesus say it. For hundreds of years, Jewish people atoned for their sin by offering a gift at the altar. It was a transaction between the sinner and God. Then Jesus showed up and told the crowd that God was so committed to them loving one another that a sacrifice at the altar wouldn't cut it anymore. They would have to repair things between themselves first.

Since Christ's death on the cross fully paid for our sins, we are no longer required to bring literal gifts to an altar. However, we *are* still required to evaluate and deal with broken earthly relationships. These broken relationships break the heart of our heavenly Father and they steal our breathing room.

When we've been hurt by another person, our tendency is to hang on to our anger and unforgiveness. We wait until the offender circles back around to make it right or pay us back. But whether he or she does or doesn't, God asks us to forgive.

He doesn't require this simply because it benefits the person we forgive, but because it protects our hearts too. The truth is that the angst, anger, and hurt of broken relationships will leak. These emotions eventually spill over into our relationships with the most important people in our lives.

Maybe as we've looked at relationships this week, you've been thinking of a relationship that needs forgiveness… not breathing room. Maybe you'd rather skip over Jesus' comments about reconciling because forgiveness feels like too much to give or to get.

It will be hard—maybe impossible—to create breathing room in any relationship if our emotional energy is tied up in unforgiveness. So let this be the push you've been waiting for to finally repair the damage. If necessary, let a counselor walk you through the process. Your first step toward the freedom of breathing room may be finding the freedom of forgiveness.

JOURNAL YOUR THOUGHTS

....

....

....

....

....

....

BROKEN RELATIONSHIPS LEAK

When you read today's devotion, was there a specific relationship that came to mind— one in need of repair, reconciliation, or forgiveness? Write about it below.

....

....

....

....

....

....

....

....

....

....

....

....

When you think of the relationship you just noted, what feelings bubble up and potentially leak out? Check all that apply or write your own responses.

☐ Unresolved anger   ☐ Lack of confidence   ☐ Anxiety

☐ Resentment   ☐ Loneliness   ☐ Sadness

☐ Fear of abandonment   ☐ Jealousy   ☐ Guilt

☐ Low self-esteem   ☐ Indignation   ☐ ....

What are some steps you can take to begin repairing this damaged relationship?
Example: Open the lines of communication by sending her a friendly text message.

....

....

....

....

....

....

....

....

....

> WHEN I AM AFRAID, I PUT MY TRUST IN YOU. IN GOD,
> WHOSE WORD I PRAISE–IN GOD I TRUST AND AM NOT
> AFRAID. WHAT CAN MERE MORTALS DO TO ME?
>
> *Psalm 56:3–4*

If you're like me, fear may not be an emotion you naturally relate to. Fear is reserved for scary movies, for trying new things, for public speaking. Fear isn't part of my daily life.

Or is it? Jesus' most repeated command in all the Bible is *fear not.* Why was he so hung up on fear?

To answer that, let's think back to the way we justify adding more to our already packed calendars. *I'm afraid if I don't say yes, they won't ask me again.*

Or to the way we justify our spending. *I'm afraid if I don't get one, too, people will think I don't have good taste.*

Or to the way we justify ourselves to our loved ones. *I'm afraid if I don't do it, someone else will have to pick up the slack.*

Ladies, fear is a part of our daily lives. Every time we're afraid of missing out, falling behind, or letting a friend down, we're letting fear call the shots. As long as we let these fears bully us around, we'll never have the breathing room we crave.

Jesus wants us to trust him instead. Our *"No, not this time"* leaves room for him to provide for us in unexpected ways. And do you know what else we get? Peace, contentment, rest, joy, and freedom from regret. That sounds pretty great, doesn't it?

Life really is better with *breathing room*.

JOURNAL YOUR THOUGHTS

....

....

....

....

....

....

....

....

As long as we let these fears bully us around, we'll never have the breathing room we crave.

WRAPPING UP

As we finish our time together, let's capture a few takeaways.

Which of the fears we've talked about is the most challenging for you?

☐ Fear of Missing Out

☐ Fear of Not Mattering

☐ Fear of Falling Behind

☐ Fear of Disappointing Others

Is there a Scripture verse we've looked at over the last 28 days that would help you combat that fear? If so, write or draw it here.

What is the first step you will take to create breathing room in your time, money, or relationships?

Example: I will cancel the subscription/membership I'm not really using anyway.

....

....

....

Write down one takeaway from this study that you'd like to remember moving forward.

....

....

....

FOR I AM THE LORD YOUR GOD
   WHO TAKES HOLD OF YOUR RIGHT HAND
AND SAYS TO YOU, DO NOT FEAR;
   I WILL HELP YOU.

Isaiah 41:13

NOTES

NOTES